Lines of Desire

Lines of Desire

Paul Dawson

PUNCHER & WATTMANN

First published in 2025
Published by Puncher and Wattmann
PO Box 279
Waratah NSW 2298

https://www.puncherandwattmann.com
web@puncherandwattmann.com

ISBN   978-1-923099-47-0

Cover design by David Musgrave
Typesetting by Morgan Arnett
Printed by Lightning Source International

NATIONAL
LIBRARY
OF AUSTRALIA
A catalogue record for this work is available from the National Library of Australia

For Vanessa, Max, and Milly

Contents

IN THEORY

#Emergence

to turn /
        to the sky, a sulphurous crest
of bird flight / the recursive
kernel
        of a story in the making

to piece together, from effect to cause, from flight
to wing, a shutter of time, to now unwind

Newton's watch, clouds rotating with the
swivel of fingertip, that kernel dropped

adopted by the loam, a line of code, a rogue
equation, numbers spiralling, the rapid dispersal

of roots, viral affects, shock of the soul
accumulating intensities, unpatterned

        across hashtags / a convergence

of birds, in the expanding shape of a letter
code proliferating

        a blink / of language / of
        twittering

phosphorescent tendrils unrooted
flocks wheeling in the sky, no leader

no origin
       of a story in the making

Lines of Desire

The movement of a narrative, some will tell you,
can be charted on a graph. To begin with

there are trees and their uncomplicated growth. There
is one's life and that's what life is. If you listen closely

you can hear the granules of coffee sliding from the spoon
to the bottom of the plunger. And then

something happens. The line of the graph
begins to curve upwards, like an eyebrow of doubt,

like a bird contemplating flight. The something is desire –
it cannot be any more specific than that.

Like the arc from her smoking fingertips
to a mouthful of lips, the way you watch water

climbing up the inside of your treasured, treasured tea cup,
this movement has consequences, rising like steam –

follow the line, watch desire break against itself
at the peak of the curve, the email that should not

have been sent, that had to be sent
as if the story was only in your mind.

And then the slow decline, or perhaps the collapse
it may be nothing, it could be madness, it could be

a sparrow's whisper on the edge of your skin.
Either way, there is the unravelling –

but how can one wrap up desire? The moment
when one is blasted into enthralment

one shivering soul, the glimpse of a foot,
her voice on the raining street, a hint

of the other way out.

Fictionality

Can one create a world just by referring to it?
Can I conjure, with words alone, that morning

known by no-one, when you climbed from
my window, grazing your leg on the way, and

I found you, walking barefoot across the grass
out of the sunrise, your eyes the impossible blue

of the horizon, where the sky shivers into the water
and we watched the lake, and the blue of last night's dress

settled into my bed, your head on my chest, your body
an indirect speech act, telling my hands what to do

with silent, dry breaths: 'How could you know I love that?'
And here is the abyss, this impossible world

of romantic bliss, of nightly fictions, where I kiss
each one of your performative selves to the core

like the apple in my hand that your teeth consumed
bite by bite, as you leaned forward, eyes opening

the night, juices alive down my fingers, our selves
unravelling, my speech undone.

Declaration of the Rights of Rights

All rights are born equal.
Some are more equal than others.
I have a right to get married
you have the right to carry a gun.
It is my right to watch porn, free
from persecution, and your right
to call me racist when I complain
about Asians who spit

but you won't call me racist, for I have asserted
my right to minority status. I invoke my Asian side
– the one that got me anthologized –
although my other side regards me as a hoax.

Freedom of religion is a right, and your beliefs
should not be compromised: no work on holy days
and no baking cakes for gays. Secular beliefs don't count
because human rights are articles without faith.

It is my right to say 'the science is not settled'
if I don't like the science. It is your right to reject
biological determinism, before accepting
the science of the gay gene.
We used to choose our sexual preference
to challenge heteronormal dominance
now desire is decided at birth, and all that's left is love.

But freedom of choice is everyone's right –
home maker, sex worker, dole bludger, asylum seeker

all lifestyle choices, right? Like a beachside property
like a Tinder swipe, like seven brands of beans
on the supermarket shelf. It is our right to sack
our prime minister, to decide how my taxes are spent
and our right to choose private services
– schools, health insurance, utilities and banks –
that's what the public wants
although privacy seems to have become
a renewable source of terror.

Metadata retention is a violation of my privacy
but leaking the content of your emails is a public
service, for people have the right to know
your sexual predilections and your obnoxious private rants
and we all have the right to litter the global aviary
with 280 characters of illiterate birdsong
like nightingales in the dark, cheering our own solitude:
they are right, you are wrong; you are right, they are left.

Everyone has the right to come here, by air or by sea
we are the land of empathy: it is our right to tow you
out of our waters, because we would hate to see you drown.
It is your right to condemn the hijab in other countries
for veiling the rights of women, and celebrate it here
as a symbol of religious freedom.

If you disapprove of what I say
I defend to the death your right
to carpet-bomb minorities
with brittle-boned words. Everyone
has the right to take offence
even white men, even the centre

as the margins close in.

Men have rights too, especially the nice ones
who never send dick pics, and the reasonable ones
who would be on your side if only you realized
that equality has gone too far.

It is my right to buy cage eggs; it is your right
to abort your foetus. It is your body, not God's
but strangers on the bus have the right
to handle your pregnant stomach
like a piece of fruit, because the life inside
is the moment of ensoulment that belongs to us all.

Every child has the right to a mother and a father
or a mother and a mother, or a father and a father
or a mother, or a father, and an achievement award
at assembly, and a role in the school play.
Some have the right to be special. Not 'special' special
but gifted and talented special, even profoundly so
like poets, all of whom have the right to be funded
and sold in bookshops.

TV stations have no right to advertise junk food
in the midst of our obesity crisis. I am not calling anyone fat:
fat is a health issue, not an aesthetic judgement.
Call me skinny, though, tell me I am skin and bones
tell me I need to eat more while you poke at my ribs.

It is your right to claim disabled status
because you have anxiety when assignments are due.
Like terror alerts, your disability can be upgraded

in times of crisis. And I have the right to be alarmed
when you write lay instead of lie, or verse
instead of versus, or cliche instead of clichéd.
Call me a grammar nazi, if you like, but once
you invoke Hitler, you have lost the argument.

My Chinese student has the right to follow me after class
and ask me about my ethnicity, for he is rightfully confused:
I look Asian, but my name is not, and my "English is so good"
but my white hairdresser cannot ask me where I am from.
Her curiosity is bigotry. I am from Sydney
so why would I care about my mother's country?

My right to say 'I', and to have it mean something
does not make this a lyric poem. It's not me, it's you.
Misogyny should be banned, but misanthropy is my right.
Some of my best friends could be homophobes
and sometimes you just don't know
whether to laugh, or to nod, or to cringe.

You have a right to die before you lose yourself –
plugged and monitored and wheezing into the
squeak of a nurse's shoe. You do not wish to suffer
without dignity, like the animals bred, captive and lightless
to be brought down with a knife for the last
of last night's supper. Ask me now
and I will help you go
gentle into that good night.

Cabbages have rights. I march in support of cabbages.
But when, with wilting cardboard placard
I reach the police barricade, that phalanx of the state,

and bodies surge with the grammar of plural pronouns
amidst the goading cameras, the tinny megaphones,
the silly slogans and the whiff of hysteria
I don't know whether to turn left or right.

This is the long twentieth century, the century of rights:
the wrongs of the past will be made right
the guillotine will drop like a lion from a rifle shot
on tumbrils full of bigotry
we will soak the anthropocene with rights
we will be at one with the earth and the Other
eight billion snowflakes melting with the ice caps
we will all be ourselves, for everyone has the right to be you
and the towers are still burning, and refugees
keep drowning, and still we are yearning
to be right.

The Men Who Hate Clementine Ford

Everyone knows one of them, the men who are #notallmen –
They are the ones who have no opinion
just facts and considered views, which they cling to
like a real estate agent to a slice of ocean
who fantasize about swooping down on a vortex
of social media feminism, and dispelling its force
with a single tone-deaf injection of reason, like:
'are you aware that men are statistically more likely
to be assaulted' or 'funny that no-one wants to discuss
male suicide rates', lamenting Clementine's swear words
and pitting rational debate against hysteria
as if explaining the mechanics of a carburetor

They are the ones who take it personally
like a kid who thinks his sister got a bigger
serve of ice-cream. Who won't recognize
the behaviour Clementine condemns
because it doesn't come from them
because they love women, their boss is a woman
and they always leave the toilet seat down.
Who squall about equality as they brandish their
hashtag syllogisms, as if feminism were a
false premise because it does not attend
to the rights of men, and how dare she

post a man's private message for all to see
the man who writes: 'You should be raped
you fucking man-hating feminazi', before
pointing out that she is too ugly to be raped

as if to be raped could also be a compliment
reserved for an attractive Tinder date
the man who utters pig, dog, slut, cunt with red-eyed relish
as if each noun possessed a natural equivalence
whose private words sit nestled to the right
of his profile picture, where he smiles
with cheeks pressed to his two daughters

And when I stare at these men and their belligerent eyes
set in a frozen Facebook smirk, I wonder
how deeply their male gaze penetrates
what they see when they look into the eyes
of their wives while they thrust inside them.
What do they think when those daughters
grow into their limbs? Would they rather protect
their girls from women like Clem or men like them?

They are the men who think women can't be funny
who assess a woman's body as if it were a work in progress
an architectural draft of their dream holiday home
who are incensed by Clementine's red lipstick
because her smile is not theirs to own
because they hate the idea of her, the idea of a woman
who renders them irrelevant by giving zero fucks
who speaks their unspoken assumptions, inviting them
to prove her right with every toxic rebuttal

They are the man in the bar who plants
his fat keys on the table and stands
with a thumb hooked over his belt
drinking his beer in slow, measured draughts
who wants the women chatting near him

to feel the weight and heat of his presence
who thinks it an affront if his boozy desire
is not acknowledged, yet takes offence if it is
because he was just trying to be friendly
who thinks his reflex quotidian leer is a compliment
because his desire needs to be legitimized
and could be, with a simple titter
or a smooth palm on his forearm
so just fucking lighten up, why don't you?

They are the man walking towards me
on the footpath, on a clear blue day
who will size me up and then bunch
his doughy shoulders, and keep going
gun-barrel straight, eyes aimed at the edge
of my temple, like a misfired gaze
inviting the collision, daring me
to be the sort of man
who hates Clementine Ford.

Thanks for the poems, Covid 19

Here's me, face-masked in a supermarket
swamped by white people, who are
angry all over again about the yellow peril
now an invisible airborne enemy speaking in tongues
through the inscrutable hospital-blue fabric
that obscures my features, that signals its silent intent
while I peer at the shelves, ensconced in the conch-shell

of my mask – until the bald, wobbly-eyed face of a
Woolworth's worker appears suddenly beside me
and barks: "Social distancing still applies in here!"
Oh sorry, what was I doing? SOCIAL DISTANCING
STILL APPLIES IN HERE he repeats, as if I can't hear
as if English escapes me, as if this is groundhog day
as if his words were a talisman to keep the threat at bay.
Yes, I say, but I don't know what I was doing?

And then, from behind, a woman's voice chimes in
to explain that she had complained because I
was blocking her path, now averting her gaze
as she swerves her trolley past, and I am left
with my own trapped breath, watching the worker
move on to stack shelves within hugging distance
of a white couple, within a whisper of their faces
as they contemplate trays of beef mince. I refrain
from repeating his talisman back to him

because really I want to scream it hysterically in his face
because I take it personally, because I'm not from, and have
never been, to China, because I know that's the wrong response
and maybe this had nothing to do with race anyway
and why the fuck did I wear this mask in the first place?
And I can't help but think of Pauline Hanson, circa the turn of the
    millennium
and all the incidents like this, which I thought had been eradicated

as if the trope of Asian contagion that lay dormant
while Islamic terrorism helped fashion Hanson's comeback
has now been revived in a virulent new strain
that cannot be warded off by hoarding toilet paper
for this behaviour is every bit as Australian
as our coming together to battle the bushfires
that tear across the nation, and to be Asian-Australian
in a pandemic is – like hoarding – to be suddenly

un-Australian, where one minor encounter can unmask
the searing loss of belonging, the sense of
impotence, the persistent second-guessing
of one's own thoughts, that typically present
as asymptomatic on all those inscrutable faces.

#auspol

aspirational voter
don't fuck with the tax system –
because even though you hate rich bastards
one day, you could be one of them
I mean, you never know

Liberal voter
don't let them take your money
you work hard – without any
handouts – and you certainly
wouldn't call yourself rich
              but yes, let the gays marry

progressive voter
secular kindness in a daily struggle
against the blindness of privilege
we are all the same
pronouns: us / them

conservative voter
you can't even fucking say
what you think anymore
around these humourless luvvies.
You have rights too, now that the margins
are oppressing you

swing voter #1
when you watch the telly
which one of their smug mugs
annoys you the least?

inner city voter
they do it tough out in the bush
but at least they have gardens –
here it's just a filter bubble of
terrace houses, cafes and apartments
with only algorithms and a line of traffic
to keep the suburbs at bay

Labor voter
once were workers
shirts begrimed with elbow grease
heaving at the picket lines
now –
      wait, who are we?

independent voter
scattergun protest vote or boutique cause?
what makes you different
is what makes the difference

Green voter
science is sexy again
like a Tinder date: swipe left
and we're all slowly burning
in the dark satanic mills

swipe right, and it's better to reign
in hell than serve in parliament

either way, our children will
soon be seeking asylum
on another planet

asylum seeker
a weather vane
for our nation's fears
or failures

teal voter
A woke in sheep's clothing?
Or just rich enough to care about
your grandkids' future
while angsting about raising
the minimum wage

swing voter #2
as the country lists
from left to right, listen
to all the sales pitches
and check your balance
like a moody pendulum

non-voter
I mean, they're all fucked.

aussie voter
spills sauce from a democracy sausage
over greasy fingers and onto
the school ground, where it sizzles in the sun
like blood on the streets in some
faraway revolution

#auspol
how good is Australia?

So Woke

So woke you set your internalised alarm
for the crack of prejudice, the false dawn
of consciousness, and wondered why folks
would have a problem with kindness
with empathy and fairness and vigilant
awareness of the strangling breath of oppression

So woke you saw hope in the tipping point
of BLM iconography: Colin Kaepernick
taking a knee echoed cruelly
in that other nine-minute knee pressed
to the back of a neck as a nation
choked on a pandemic

So woke you never slept, checked
your privilege and rejected
the epithet, called it meaningless
because you never use it
that one-time clarion call twisted
into a catch-all adjective of dismissive
fear, a parody of progressiveness
used as a cudgel by trolls and moderates
alike to bludgeon your sensitivities

So woke you worked from home in your
bespoke office and bemoaned those
who don't follow the science
as your groceries got delivered
by workers on the roam from Local
Government Areas of concern

but you know this, of course, you have
completed the cultural reflexivity courses
you have combed your soul for micro-
aggressions and casual racism, opened
every Zoom meeting with an acknowledgement
of your own complicity, tweeted your pronouns in solidarity
amidst the cat-calls of a call-out culture
that baulks at women asserting
their embodied identity

So woke you climbed into the trope
of the white woman editor with a tote
bag and a token sensitivity reader, that
symbol of scorn for left and right
that scapegoat for the failure of diversity
searching for stories that only others can tell

but you can tell that there is no unwoking now
because what is the alternative in the wake
of a wave of resentment engulfing
the world, a spite-lashed backlash
like a tsunami stripping palm trees
from a beachside boulevarde and
drowning us in the slumbering reflux
of centuries of undead white men.

Connectivity

snapchat flashback / instagram spammed & user banned / spasm
of ambient chasm / an echo chamber / of we too and not u / click here

share there / feed me / news now / if you like / update life / a daily
grindr / right-swiped / tinder-box of / trolls triggered in twittering

tongues of wildfire spreading hahhaahaha data
mining to confirm your bias and buy us / advertising

the algorithmic revolution of the here and now / outrage
recycled / love affairs upcycled / news cycle spiralled / into

youtube wombs / breeding rabbits out of / scrolling habits
your mom sharing baby showers / while conspiracies flower

next door / in the darkest corners / of 4chan fanning flames
of discord / games streaming / live tears and

gunshot wounds / in first-person / active shooter face to
face / with facebook ads as / bodies twitch in / an emptied parler

you reddit here first / did your research / before reaching for / a tumblr
full of hashtagged / viruses to influence us / bot by bot / as the clock tik

toks to / a mic-drop / post of post-truth / posturing mis-
information / if you blink & dis / information is in

nobody's pinterest just / the story of your feels / in reels of loves &
likes / & trending spikes of AI fakes & / kneejerk flights into bluesky
nights

The Teams Scream

There are already four people in the meeting
join now or hurl yourself into the abyss
un-slash your microphone and your video
like a big reveal, and abandon all hope
ye who enter here

this grid of faces casting glances
                              askance
across a split screen
like a nightmare reprisal
of *The Brady Bunch* credits

silhouettes unwrapped
from the warping portal of portable
backgrounds, humblebrag apologizing
for cats materializing on laps, amidst
twisted nods to off-screen ghosts

Admit to lobbying guests for
the sake of usefulness, the cymbal clash
of other people's notifications
the inanities popped into the chat
the emojis, the emojis

That self-muted colleague
all eye-brows and animated vowels
spilling silence into the ether
like Munch's *The Scream* on Ritalin
until they spy the flurry of fingertips
jabbing theatrically at earholes

then stillness –
the world tilting on a desktop
colleague reaching out of shot
nostrils filling the space where their face once
was and you are messaging Virgil
asking how many circles are left, lol

Name = Compatibility Mode

11.30 - 11.45am - I am / your name
an empty parenthesis, a passage of thought
dispersed in <o:OfficeDocumentSettings> ![endif]
normal view / use to > invoke cognitive frame
<w:ValidateAgainstSchemas/> to narrate code in lyric
<IgnoreMixedContent> <DoNotPromoteCausality/>
</w:LidThemeAsian> <w(hite): Compatibility> Dawson
<LidThemeComplexScript> recursive patterns
of emergent language / to escape your parent-name
UseAsianBreakRules/> of cultural identity
<SplitPgBreakAndParaMark/> run-on line/free
verse = prose = code diffusion <w:DontFlipMirrorIndents/>
of the self </Compatibility w/Other
DefUnhideWhenUsed = "true" DefSemiHidden = "post-truth"
UnhideWhenUsed = "false" logic of social media post
your "true" Name = autofiction / LsdException red pill
episode or White = "false" Name = "Light List Accent 1"/> Asian
Name = "Revision" of self/> multicultural format = "true"
Name = "Intense Quote"/> Unquote
Exception Locked = "false" biography born Sydney 1972
Name = "Dark List Accent 1"/> oriental cunning
Name = "Colorful Grid Accent 1"/> character
Name = hybrid identity (asian themed)
Name = "Light Shading Accent 3"/> white wash
Name = rigid designator / or nonreferential entity
Name = nobody's story = true because it made you feel
a sympathetic identification: Name = "Intense Emphasis"/>
Name = "Book Title"/>
Name = "Bibliography"/>

Name locked = "false" Priority = clickbait

mso-style-noshow: yes; mso-style-parent;

pagination: widow-orphan;

death of the author = birth of birth of

<metaphor> font-family: Name your

</style> <![endif] StartFragment

EndFragment

General discussion

Indicative

The blue of a curl that nominates
a cloud, its cumulative presence
an apparent artifice saturated
with naïveté, with the petal gentleness
of a sky in transition – streak of
smooth colour illuminating
the meandered edge from nimbus

to ether, and then after –
a sudden sunken heralding
of yesterday's clause
contraction of an eye birthed
in the image of what was to come.

ON THE PAGE

Ten Poetic Commandments

1.

You shall have no other gods before Me. I am your Muse, who brought you out of the land of prose, out of the prison house of narrative. I am the breath of a pagan deity, I am the white throat of a Renaissance lover, I am the buried self, for you to discover. I am you, who were born and not made.

2.

You shall not make for yourself a poem about the little mindless epiphanies that emerge from the quotidian rhythms of your life, or a poem that righteously demonstrates your empathy for marginalized identities. You shall not reflexively meditate on your writing process, or the simple clarity of the sky framed by a stanza. Nor shall you unfurl a concatenation of paratactic phrases to show the labile profundity of your thought emerging from the cracks between caesuras, semi-colons; dashes – & / slashes.

3.

You shall not take the name of the Lord your Muse in vain, for the Muse has a long memory, and you will be visited by pompous classical allusions and abstract nouns that dance in the light of the nation's soul.

4.

Remember the writing day, to keep it holy. Six days you shall fuck around and pretend to write by taking long Wordsworthian perambulations through stringybark trees, and jotting Dickinsonian fragments on envelopes, and 'finding' poems by putting line breaks in instruction manuals, or cutting and pasting google searches, in between editing your biographical note and retweeting poetry memes. And on the seventh day you shall write a draft, and it shall be crap, but there will be a little mag out there, somewhere, probably on the web, that shall take your work – and if not, you shall post it on your blog, and call it forthcoming, and hover for the next six days, waiting for comments.

5.
Honour Sappho and Homer, that your legacy may be long in its reach. Honour yourself too, with libations. Though you walk through the valley of the shadow of the figurative, you shall not fear obscurity.

6.
You shall not murder to dissect. Such is the province of critics and creative writing teachers. Give them the rosy-dawned finger. You give birth, you create.

7.
You shall not commit hoaxology. Do not pretend to be Asian and write a poem about making noodles with your grandmother. Split the infinite. Watch it curve like a question mark over the post-Language enjambments of contemporary verse. Also, you shall not spend your Australia Council funds on prostitutes.

8.
You shall not steal another poet's words, and you shall not misquote T.S. Eliot, nor invoke the language of pastiche and appropriation, to rationalize your dearth of imagination.

9.
You shall not bear false witness against your neighbour's doggerel. You love her work, especially the early stuff.

10.

You shall not covet your fellow poet's publications, especially their pretty chapbook covers and their selected works so visibly, so palpably on display at Gleebooks; you shall not covet your fellow poet's reviews, nor his or her grant (for you eschew the devil's pact of the public teat), nor her female editor whose stilettos ripped through your dreams, nor his transgender lover, nor her writer's retreat in a villa in Italy, nor his ten thousand dollar prize money collected from the entry fees of a thousand false dreamers, nor their Twitter followers, Wikipedia entries, well-attended readings, and invitations to appear at the Writers Festival on a panel entitled "Does Anybody Read Poetry Anymore? (Because They're Sure as Shit Still Writing it)." For you know that the meek shall inherit the anthologies, and all that matters is you, your Muse, and the blinking cursor, as you await the second coming.

Contemplating Dumplings

I am contemplating parcels of white
contentment, watching them steam

under paper lanterns, their faces trickling with
multiculturalism as they tuck into platefuls

of dumplings and wonton, of noodles that slip
from wooden chopsticks, and I wonder –

if I can beckon the neglected heritage
of my second self, the ancestral half

masked by my name, now piqued
by the rising sharpness of chilli and soy

could I release, with one inspired bite, an Asian-
Australian poem into the lantern-lit night?

A poem of yearning confusion, of desire
for a homeland I never knew, of a journey

from steamer to Sydney hawker-style alleyway
pluming with the spices of my mother's childhood

a poem plump with meaning that a generation
of schoolkids will be invited to decipher

for their HSC standard English exam, Module A:
Language, Identity and Culture

salivating as they trace the trope of dumplings
which oscillates from the literal to the figurative

as if wobbling between the chopsticks
and the suspicious lips of a table full of *gwai lo*

those soft parcels of white contentment
now stained by the dark soy of a hybrid identity –

perhaps this will help me in the search
for my own becoming, a third way

to the front of the queue
for another serve of dumplings.

How to be an Asian Australian

1. To Asian or not Too Asian

If I were a contestant on *Masterchef*
What would my signature dish be?

Would I wow the judges with the clean, hearty
jié guā tong my mother used to ladle forth

into misty hot bowls she shared with my sister
as the silkiness of her steamed fish bloomed

from under the cloche of a wok's broken lid?
Or would it be the reliably tender lamb chops

with boiled veggies she comforted my father with?
I, of course, ate neither, surviving on a diet of picky

blandness, and eating hot chips through childhood trips
to the homeland. So what story do I have to tell?

How will I get to share with Melissa Leong
 – that paragon of multiculturalism –

 a poignant crinkle-faced moment
of Asian-Australian recognition

where I come to know that now I belong
where I become the identity Australia wanted all along?

2. A Community of Asians

Do I choose to be or not to be
Asian Australian? Not just an Aussie
but an Asian one, my identity spiced
with a slice of multicultural exotica
to help me stand out from the crowd –
maybe not the crowd where it means to be half
an Aussie, a provisional one, one who should
go home to where I never came from
but the crowd that lauds diversity, exhorting me
to be not only me but part of a community
of Australians with a difference: an Asian-

Australian community, where as long as
you have a hint of epicanthus, as long as you
or your mother, or someone in your family
has some connection to some country in a continent
east of the west and north of down under
you could get together over a bowl of noodles
sauce-laden and unravelled onto a plate
with any other member of this innate
collective to share your lived experience

like a flock of pigeons or a pride of lions –
a community of Asians, identities sutured together
in a multicultural melange with your own
demographic heft, your own anthologies
full of bloodlines and storylines, your own bylines
and voting lines and diasporic lines of flight

landing you here in this community within
a land of sweeping plains and orientalist strains
wondering why there seems to be no need for
a European Australian community, whether it could be
because *they* don't all look alike to a white
community who needs no community
because, after all, we are all Aussies, right?

3. Not all White

Perhaps I could identify as white – yes, that's right, a yt
one of the wipopo. I know, my skin is the colour
of a browning lemon, and my eyes read like a slant
rhyme. I know my hair is as black as those eyes
as black as a fossil fuel from the dark ages
when I was called a chink and things like that at school.
You wouldn't know it, though, from my name or my voice
you would think I was white, and you would be at least half right.

Perhaps you read this as a sign of internalised racism
perhaps you think that I am a dinosaur of assimilation
a second-generation, Australian-born, half-breed
born into whiteness and afraid of difference?

You would be just like that Anglo housewife after the matinee
session of "Fresh Off the Boat," Belvoir street Theatre
who said she felt so sorry for my character because (like me)

he had no connection with his heritage. Well, thank you, *gwai mui*
for sharing your vision of multiculturalism, but who said
I have to have a hyphenated self? If some us can rightfully

claim the exotic side of their blood ties, why can't I
claim the culture I was born into? Tea and scones
and footy and cricket and meat pies and the canon
of English literature, where you can be white without having
to write about it, like Wordsworth rambling through the lakes.

Maybe I don't want to be a billboard of hybridity, a dot point of diversity
because what's so special about the immigrant past of my Othered half?
because, you know, it's okay to be white, because hashtag #notallwhites
because white lives matter too, so why blame us for being
stained with a privilege we never knew we even had?

So yes, I identify as white. I mean, not white
supremacist neo-Nazi white – not the whine-about-
quotas-and-reverse-racism white, or the pass a motion
in parliament that it really is okay to be white
but just, like ...
unmarked, invisible, out of sight white

the white I always assumed I was
until I kept getting reminded otherwise
white as all the colours on the spectrum
or the blinding light of Enlightenment
white as a blank page, white as a frozen lake
white as cooked rice, white as a steamed dumpling
white as a lonely cloud wandering
amidst a host of golden daffodils.

Dickinson's Envelope

In the Special Collections archives of Amherst college
a twenty-five year old grad student named Lizzie
ungathers the twine around those famous packets
of folded stationery, inked with lyrics of tremulous insight

her excited breath a reprise of what she assumes
would have been the inhalation of scholars before her
in this silent room. Here is the envelope on the back of which
Emily wrote a fragment of thought which editors thought

could be a lyric. Here is the imprint of a leaf on a letter
once opened by her brother. And here are her own thin fingers
cramped from the pen she has forgotten how to use.
Here she is, gathering threads, a bowerbird in the archives.

She knows Emily was a bluebird, although she has never
heard one sing. She writes poetry too. She knows she is no
Genius! – but she too feels the throb of life
and death, the need for her verses to be alive,

to have breathed. She struggles, more than Emily
ever could have, with that long dark horizon her lines
will never breach, the barrenness of her own breath
as she flounders in quotidian musings on teacups

and friendship, in compilations of abstract nouns
typing thoughts which she can never make her own
straight onto the computer, the screen a palimpsest
the cursor her guillotine.

Imagine if from this envelope slipped
a handwritten recipe for New England bread
its inky presence yearning through the centuries.
Could this be a poem, yet unversified?

Two Quarts Flour – a single Yeast Cake
Water – Blood warm! – and Sugar –
Let the loaf breathe unshriven
On a Syllable – till you spy
The Birds come picking

What if she slipped one of her own imperfect offerings
into that envelope? Would it be discovered, she wonders
to become poem number 1776 in another edition, lineated
to the accent of Emily's singular trill? She writes poetry too.

Perhaps, in years to come, a fevered hoaxology expert would cart
her hard drive, her corroded memory sticks, from a cardboard box
in her sister's attic, to the university's windowless IT room
in search of missing drafts. Would trawl her emails

to her graduate advisor, to her family in Australia
google her posts on poetry blogs, her Facebook blurts, in search
of a philosophy, a lesbian lover, a poem that might
have been, before her digital trail evaporates

in the vacuum of cyberspace, where no one can hear you scream.
Maybe then someone would know that she breathed
that once she was alive, aching for a line of flight
from Dickinson's envelope into the clear blue of birdsong.

Musing

1. Untitled
When a poet falls in love, desire is
apostrophized in a spring of words

the verses emerge from an urge to court
and the poem begins as a *lettre d'amour*.

But in order to be written, it must be cease to be
about the lover, about you. The impossible blue

of that morning becomes material
for the ruthless, as the poet falls in love again

with shining words. It is the only way
for the letter to become a poem

that alchemical cleaving of selves
in the reader that is not you.

2. Acknowledgements
When a scholar falls in love
critical concepts take on new resonance.

To focalize means something else.
Possible worlds acquire a quiver of urgency;

the *lingua franca* of the field is transmuted
into a private language for two.

You know how it is. Ideas of self and other
take shape in a bibliography

and every reference is about you
for you, to you.

3. Forthcoming
When this lover falls, everything cascades
into the singularity of your flesh

beneath my fingers, as they trace
down your back the unscored rhythm

from neck to natal cleft
that brought us to the edge

of together. It never ends
this rewriting, even when it is over.

Reading Hopkins

Because of you, for you, I am reading Hopkins
For how your voice wrings his words
From within, no worst than sin – how
This sonnet of God-lashed despair
Grips me, socket to bone, on your tongue
Like an erotic shock, a secular moan. Listen.

I am listing. You have sprung me
You have wrung from me all yearning
For other than you, for all that is not
Your birthmarked flesh, or the pitch of your heart
Which I know roils for me, across our ravished
Hours, like "The Wreck of the Deutschland" roils
On my tongue, right now, clockwise toward the sublime.

Songbirds after the Lyric

From the window, that casual warble
and chatter of unseen birds, clustered
somewhere amongst the leaves,
like an occasional question mark
punctuating the crisp prose of
the morning light, now enjambed

with their lines of flight. I try to scribe
the range of their avian dialogue –
that fast paced clatter against the air
their drawn out call-outs from branch
to fence, those deep inquisitive squalls
those melancholy cries scrawled

across the dawn-scrubbed sky.
A futile exercise in ham-fisted mimickry
to utter this untranslatable echo in my tone-deaf ear
of birds whose names I don't even know.

Coleridge and Shelley had the nightingale
and the skylark, Dickinson the bluebird
Hopkins the windhover and woodlark –

but why try to personify?
I resist their apostrophising and
content myself with eavesdropping
on the wordless lyric exchange
of these anonymous backyard birds.

Triptych

print poet
days of blackened depth
that none can fathom

performance poet
to be melancholic/is not such a frolic/you can't
skip the topic/like picking olives from a
martini/there's no houdini/out of yourself

instapoet
never forget, it's okay to be you

My Life as a Best Selling Poem

I am a sage for the internet age
self-made, selfie-laden
designed to assuage
your life-sick hearts with a quick
stanza of solipsistic wisdom
ready to post at a moment's notice

people flock to me, they swoon
as I sway to my own words
of self-love body worth in
cupfuls of clauses recited
with Pinteresque pauses
like a churchbell
in the wind, intoning
me, me, me, but don't

blame me for I am
but the viral messenger
for this mass psychosis
of the muse

epoemjis

hieroglyphs of affect
thumbed out by the millions

😂 😍 😭

our own digital lingua franca - 😳
the art of virtual 🫣 physiognomy

- facial recognition
(epoemji #1)

in a station, on messenger

the apparition 👻 of these faces 🫥 on your screen

pixels on a slick, black phone 📱

- (epoemji #2)

emojism 🐌
an emotional and 🥒 ironic complex
in an instant update 👆

👍 Like   ◯ Comment

- (epoemji #3)

ugghhh it doesn't matter what you think

that's how i feel 😣

– dissociation of sensibility
(epoemji #4)

my poem is fu
~~funny~~
my poem is fucked 😥

– autocorrect
(epoemji #5)

lol

like rain  on your

wedding day

🙄

– lol
(epoemji #6)

Evolutionary Verse

variations on a poetic sequence
must adapt to the line

break, a natural selection of
the fittest syllable, mutating

under the code of the
half-breath pause

We are Data

We are   [chiefly in *plural.*]
data are   [as a mass noun]
our days are
numbered
into spiking graphs of
keyword searches and browser
purchases, the collective lyric
of our anonymised selves
extrapolated from an absurdist performance
of techno-capitalism, a correlation
of digits, a rapid blizzard of blinks
like a poet counting syllables
in a line of code, mining raw souls for

                          [large sets of]

            Data-ism / I am
the original datum, the first
extracted resource, called into being
by your algorithmic hypothesis
distilled to a profile by your
programmable bias, I share myself
for every datum belonging to me as good belongs to you
predicting me, revealing to me   [an item of]
the invisible design of my own desires
and habits, beyond the residue   [chiefly numerical]
of my self, the eleventh syllable
in our unpatterned pentameter   [information]

Submittable

Thank you for your submission
We look forward to reading it

Thank your for your interest
We cannot survive without it

Your work has been received
Your work is in-progress

We will get back to you, if we can
To let you know how busy we have been

How many manuscripts we have seen
Like delirious skies drowning in rivers

We are grateful for the opportunity
To have waded through the slush pile

And plucked you from obscurity
For a moment we paused to ponder your style

But really, and don't take this personally
It's just not for us, it's not quite right

It's not that we think your work is shite
It's just that we know what we like

And we would like to wish you the very best
Yes, the very best, in placing this elsewhere.

Afterthought

Like a word that might
speak to fever and light
so suggestive in its green
its lambent probing of leaves

that this whole thing could be a crisis
of the moment, of something
that could be a poem, but since that
can't be defined, can only be felt

like the texture of grass in your dreams
the moment when Ashbery opens your self
and mental post-it notes go missing
like socks, and you don't know what

you want to say, if you want
to say, because you cling to that lambency
when sunlight shrivels from leafy veins
like a dying gas lamp, like a classical allusion

that same light on her limbs, but as if lit from within
flesh as smooth and warm as stones
left in the sun, although pliant, an exposed thigh
like a word that might, so you go ahead

and you touch

IN THE FLESH

Bio-diversity Note

Moving through this climate-fucked world
in a racialised body made Australian by birth
made Asian by an askance glance of the white gaze
claimed hybrid by the pride of identity politics
and anthologized by diversity ticks, half-

marginalized by ancestry but privileged by class
announcing my gender as a Cartesian metaphor
floundering upon pronouns as I fall
through age groups that keep ratcheting up
like bracket creep, feeling seen

as the patchwork of my belonging comes into being
through coordinates of place, race, sex-
uality, mobility and brain chemistry to forge this
teeeming bio-diversity, this identity sales pitch
for a submission checklist like census day come early

The Virus and I

What counts for a person now, as we
are all rendered potential vectors? What happens
to the bodies of others when they are extracted
from our orbit and flattened to liquid crystal on a laptop –
faces quarantined in grids, a mouth unclosed in a frozen utterance
while its discontinuous voice echoes from a speaker

What loss will be scored on the body as we hoard our touch?
The clamp and surge of a handshake, the loose-armed curl of
an embrace, the smack of lips unpursing against a cheekbone
the unthinking slippage and jostle of limbs in a crowd.
How long before our flesh recovers from the flinch
the recoil, the swerving berth, the hover above a surface

the interpretation of a face as it breaches the distance
searching for the life inside that only a scientist can read
a viral particle nanometres wide, too tiny for the eyes, propelled
through the air in a droplet of speech, binding to a cellular receptor
like a breathless lyric addressing you from within.

All that Matters

Unkeel from the moan
       of your biosecurity bubble
of fret and lather, of rinse
           to the bone
of school at home and work
           on the edge
and breach of park run, of hug
like homicide, maybe
           or suicide, lung-bust
gauntlet of the aisle spill
of protest slicking the streets
with change now
       your right for their right to
take another little pound of your flesh now
maybe, you know you've got it
if it makes you breathe too, your
pound on the streets, your pound and pound
and how to feel like you, yeah, in
       the hammer breath of chant
a lockdown prayer for the never all matter
and fever spread from summer to summer.

The Wreck of the Heartland

You have chosen your compass for this voyage.
It is not the fixity of the astronomer's chart –
the neck-craning gaze of the brilliant night.
It is not the arrow that aligns itself to those
distant winters in your palm. It is the ebb-tide
below you, the bloody chamber that tells you
with each rushed second that you are alive
for now. It is constant in its fickle desire.
You will pursue this course beyond the
wreck of the heartland, into the spittle of the ocean
into the blue eyes of the horizon, the slaughtering
waters beneath you. Good night,
good morning, and good night again, you say
because the electricity that sundered the sky
that once, that dawn, is enough, and all.

Speech Act

With that almost sigh
on the brink of your lips
that soft flare of pupils as if
lit by a distant aurora somewhere
behind my shoulder, the space
between us seems

a suddenly breachable abyss.
Can this hovering tension be
a wordless perlocutionary?
If I reach across the table

to the curve and drop
of your cheekbone, shaped
like a question mark
on the cusp of a promise
could this be the declarative act
that changes our world
without the need for speech?

Possible Worlds

So it was a mistake, you tell me, but my emptied hands
don't follow this logic. They know only the yearning

for the skin of your palms, the way your fingers press flat
against mine in a white lie, the colour of hotel sheets

of my t-shirt clinging to your torso, your legs bare and nothing
but the heft and curve of your shoulder under my arm

in the huddled coil of this embrace. Here desire yields
the nonsense of all explanations, chronologies spinning

awry, and the heat of your thigh is enough. In this world
your body unravelling from my arms is like a small trauma

and the mistake is to let you stand there, to not clutch you
close and conjure the intensity of those lights that soughed

in the trees on that lingering half-remembered walk
through drunken leaves, lamp-posts quivering

from the water, each one lighting a possible world
which the flesh knows cannot be winnowed.

Five Lines Can Say Only

1. Ellipsis
That moment on skype; the moment that hangs
before hanging up, a tremor along the equatorial line
a clinging gaze, fingertips quarter-raised
to lips on the precipice
of a breath, of saying it.

2. The Rhythms of Sex
Five beats in ten, your breath in stress
clamouring for the little death
in a repetition of vowels, an invocation,
an apostrophe to an absent self
beyond the horizon of my shoulder.

3. Do not Reply
Six months later and still
strands of your hair
appear in my sheets, on my clothes
like letters in the mail
for strangers who lived here before me.

You Beat Against Me

you beat against me
ocean on rock, its froth and spume a ruse
for the slow erode of the word for love
battered thing, whiplashed and withering
surprise of birdwing scrabble at the window
tremor of, trembling, glass pane a revelation
of quiet, the thought – to no-one –
that this is alone

     you beat against me
slap of solitude, flash of blame flush with
guilt from flank to face, palm on cheek-
bone, feathered tip of our child's hip
couched in the crook, the little sigh of
morning silence (before she returns to you)
child-time, chided, this tiny sigh a wordless
echo of absolute trust

     you beat against me, rusted
memory of love, hover of split, ours, spilt, unvowed
scribbled signature a blot of scattershot anger
across the bow, look of helpless, how
the pulse of your breath would fill my gasp
your vein-throb pulse from
ankle to wrist, unkissed now
life to the bone, beat against me, wear me down
make me moan for more again

and next thing

and now us / from the window in / dawn enfleshed / in breath
in breast / in lung in heart / of beat and ten and / life give down to
skin to sense / and then we lay / pressed in limb and
near to pulse / for love of rapture / before rupture
of time and tense of thigh / wrought the little, long dying
from the speechless / act unearthed in the bed of our never
our foundless ever, the promise of the yes
          – that wild yes – your dress of
blue of dawn, of dew and grass / and then the clutch of us, the
breath tug / narcotic yes, laid out of the body / the rush
from the throat, the one from two / abreast the break
of flesh-tide and crest of kiss / of limb heat, of five-beat
blood line / measured thus: the wuthering gust /

of your laugh in my /
the arch of your sole in my /
the now of you in my /
the burst of flock in your /

wingless eye when the lie / became lain, and moon strain / split the
    stress
out of the break / from the sky to the limb, the white-sheet cling
under lips / under tongue, under fingers now flung / and flown
over the known and laid out / end-stopped
except for / the longing swallow
in the veins, in the palm / under trip / under tap / and flash
of flesh hemmed to unend / the line-beat, blood-body of
skin tremor, leg shudder and / faith in flight and not of next/

We are Still in the Day

Do you wake to the crush of the ocean
too distant to hear, wondering if it is my voice

in the next room, or somewhere beyond
the rain, calling your name

the way I listen each morning
for the gathering of your limbs

that ungathers my breath, wanting
to expose the skin of your moon

to my orange sky so we can rise
together before your eyes close

to nothing but the soughing of
sheets under your feet, the ocean

across the hemisphere, there, in your ear
and here, on my lips, your name.

Becoming

First the sheer cling of the stockings, snagging
your breath as they gather momentum
transforming your legs; the catch of the bra
pulling back your shoulders, willing you
into the performance of gender
as you fill out the panties, the spread
of their lace coaxing you
the nylon slip alive on your skin
like a woman's palm fashioning curves
from the lean clay of your torso.

The wig is hot, its hair spilling, thick and
unfamiliar, over your ears, your shoulders
the foundation of this ruse coating your cheeks
with a heavy foreign blush.
You cannot stop staring at the splash of red
that your nails have become. You know
this is improbable, that you can never be
the object of your gaze, but these
accoutrements may yet trick your body
into new movements, may hush your voice
may release you from the heft of your shoulders
open out your hips, allow your mouth
to speak its confusions.

The mirror beckons. The mirror affords
the reckoning. You want to see
a stranger, you want it to be you.
Your friend is with you, your dear accomplice

in this show, who has laboured over your face
with her battery of powders and glues
who has erased and redrawn the hair of your brows
so delicately traced your lips with colour
as she tended you like no other
whose face had never been so close to yours
and which you scrutinized with a forensic desire
knowing it is the measure of your failure.
Her unmade complexion is immaculate
as white as the name you have chosen
to give voice to your yearning, the name
invented by a poet for a hoax Gaelic
epic. She accompanies you
to the reckoning, as hopeful as you.

And now you cannot speak, your hand hovering
dumbly, only a breath from your cheekbone
as you stare at the reflection of a woman
you could almost be, never more acutely aware
of the shape of your jaw, the prominence
of that original sin lodged in your throat
the *pomum Adami* you wish you could spit forth
yet transfixed, still, by the art of the possible
the lashed vulnerable eyes, framed by silver
the painted lips pursing unconsciously
at the nonreferential entity gathering inside you
ready now to inhabit your name and turn
from the mirror to her.

They, Tiresias

Tiresias lives
pronouns: he/she/they
spanning generations and identities

today / the myth distorted amidst the spread of mis-
information: what triggered his seven-year
gender transition, what blinded her
but gave them prophetic vision?

The wiki for this mythic figure has it / that he posted
a video of two ruddy-arsed conservative politicians
rutting liberally in parliamentary chambers
while on the dark web / it is said / that he
witnessed an unnatural transaction / between a bat
and a human / in a Wuhan wet market.
Either way, virality ensued, and whether
it was the Fates or the Deep State, Tiresias
was transformed into his Other.

Silenced Tiresias, seven years living as a woman
her mornings littered with catcalls as common
as birdsong, learning to grip the echo-stepped air with a key
between her knuckles / each nocturnal home-coming
habituated to a ceaseless loop of online threat and request
until she returned to maleness with newfound empathy

for the embodied experience of women. Except
'he', Tiresias, had no right to write this experience as 'I'
and so could not tell her story, only bear witness to her past

in a fictional memoir about the burden of privilege
pilloried online as blind to his own entitlement
his classical lineage in western culture

Eyeless Tiresias, reduced to a bit part provocateur / on talk show panels
quizzed on whether / he had better /orgasms as a man or a woman
or prodded / for polemical commentary on gender essentialism
did they become the gender she felt on the inside / or do we all perform
a form of drag? / before an anonymous donor on GoFundMe

granted the gift of an Other eye, a second vision, and with it
epiphanic release from history, from cultural pruriency
for they / are not / and never were / male or female
but both / and neither / at the same time.
They, Tiresias, recurring trope of liminality

now striding virus-emptied streets, riddled with the chassis
of abandoned Ubers, a city wasteland
where Eliot's miserable clerks have long ceased traipsing
from trains to the ruptured cushions of stained office chairs
so many undone by the work-from-home outsourcing rort
as businesses turn suburban kitchens into networked
open-plan offices / and atomised employees
meet mutely over blank screens / dreaming of water coolers

venturing outside only for bacchanalian release on race days
when the world tilts on the edge of a helicopter blade
selves spilling over in drunken clusters of
sway-limbed wobble / and sweat-necked jostling
as whipped horses tear around the tracks
dreaming of the day they can put humans out to pasture

Tiresias, posthuman prophet against capitalist profit
ironic consultant for corporations with a conscience
patron saint of stockmarket forecasts / data mining / and economic
    modelling
of future scenarios / and predictive analytics
Tiresias, blind seer of the sun, they who can gaze directly
into the blaze of Apollo's eye / reflected back into the sky
by a million solar panels / deflecting attention from the
unceased burning of the underworld –

@Tiresias / from motif to meme / influencer extreme
until the slow collapse of the internet that they themselves predicted
sparked by a semi-conductor shortage after the fall of Taiwan
hastened by a new Zeta variant infecting people via Zoom
and stubbornly resistant to Pfizer's anti-virus software

Tiresias, canary in the coal mine, dead from imbibing
bottled water sourced from a river tainted by mining spills
to be recycled by a start-up venture offering detoxified H_2O –
zinc and cyanide dyed pale raspberry when its stocks began to tank

Now a shade, Tiresias, addressing world leaders via video link-up
from a shaft deep within the ground, surrounded by the smoulder
of black and lumpen fuel / their sallow posthumous body swelling /
    with colour
as they kneel / like a grotesque algorithm / to lap blood from the
    shrivelled rivers:
You who raped the earth you called Mother, you don't need a seer
to tell you what you already know. Consult your clocks
it's five to midnight, and your island havens are disappearing.
Prepare your ships to join me. Heed me now, or call me Cassandra.

Lover Nature

Do I dare love you, here, amongst the vines
that climb along the limbs of trees

that twine about your thighs, alive
with twisting desire in my fingers

travelling down your skin, legs exposed
like stripped saplings in the sun

until your feet are bared, planted in the earth
amongst the roots whose path I trace

through the loam, to erupt from the grass
the gnarled arch I have yearned to touch

mother no longer – lover nature, body
without organs, lay me down

inside you now and open me up, fuck me
the way a swallow plunges in the air

the way fronds caress a branch, and slip
your shoots between my lips: tell me now

how you have responded to your plundering
with a hot screaming in the sky, your violations

denied by those who want to raze you
yet keep a patch of you to escape to

tell me how to love you beyond morality
give me consent to fuck you

without a human witness
cell deep and shorn of metaphor.

Aerial Root

tree branch or root
       tangled down from burden-bowed
              bough, a dangle of drop, collected in a knot
of threaded wood, like a dried dewdrop, a husky stalactite in stop-
                  motion stretch for
the earth, for the burnt-off petrichor, the deep, loam-fingered soil,
                       home-coming
once more – rooted branch accumulating its yearslong soar

    static upward draw, limb-thickening, into a lumbering tumble of trip
from gnarled beam, sideways to the fore, under-
    growth rupturing the grassy floor / a wooden-snaked trace across
tufted clutches / a tortoise race to far-flung trunk, layers of bark scored
by the dozen in last-century's pre-war
        anchoring / athwart the earth, unfraught, holding court

in the droop of the sun, canopied monument beckoning
            breeze-buoyed leaves asway, midday
      laying on of palms, laid on calloused bark
    column of dumb wisdom, its braille a silent call, hearkened
before the rustle of twitter, hustle-feathered embarkation

Acknowledgements

Poems in this collection have previously appeared in the following publications: "#Emergence," *Meanjin* 78.2 (2019); "Lines of Desire," *Snorkel* 12 (2010); "Fictionality," *Meanjin* 75.1 (2016); "Declaration of the Rights of Rights," *Newcastle Poetry Prize Anthology, 2016*; "The Men Who Hate Clementine Ford," *Cordite Poetry Review* 86 (2018); "Thanks for the Poems, Covid-19," *Mascara Literary Review* 26 (2021); "#auspol," *Cordite Poetry Review* 97 (2020); "Name = Compatibility Mode," *Westerly* 64.2 (2019); "Ten Poetic Commandments," *Island Magazine* 149 (2017); "Contemplating Dumplings," *Peril Magazine* 39 (2019); "Dickinson's Envelope," *Contemporary Asian Australian Poets* (Puncher & Wattmann, 2013); "Musing," *Australian Poetry Anthology* Vol. 4 (2015); "Reading Hopkins," *Contemporary Asian Australian Poets* (Puncher & Wattmann, 2013); "Songbirds after the Lyric," *Stilts* 7 (April 2020); "Triptych," *Meanjin* 81.4 (2022); "Submittable," *Cordite Poetry Review* 108 (2023); "Bio-diversity Note," *Cordite Poetry Review* 112 (2024); "The Wreck of the Heartland," *Mascara Literary Review* 20 (2017); "Possible Worlds," *Australian Poetry Journal* 1.1 (2011); "Five Lines Can Say Only," *Australian Poetry Journal* 6.2 (2016); "Lover Nature," *Covert Plants* (2018).

www.ingramcontent.com/pod-product-compliance
Lightning Source LLC
Chambersburg PA
CBHW021156090426
42740CB00008B/1110